Youth Ministry

John Woolen –
"It's not about who's right,
it's about what's right."

Abingdon Press & The Church of the Resurrection
Ministry Guides

Youth Ministry

Jason Gant
Adam Hamilton, Series Editor

ABINGDON PRESS
Nashville

YOUTH MINISTRY

This book is printed on acid-free paper.

Library of Congress Cataloging-in-Publication Data

Gant, Jason.
  Youth ministry : /Jason Gant.
     p. cm.— (Abingdon Press & the Church of the Resurrection ministry guides)
  ISBN 978-0-687-65039-2 (binding: adhesive perfect : alk. paper)
  1. Church work with youth. I. Title.

  BV4447.G35 2008
  259'.23–dc22

                                                                    2008004455

08 09 10 11 12 13 14 15 16 17—10 9 8 7 6 5 4 3 2 1
MANUFACTURED IN THE UNITED STATES OF AMERICA

Contents

Foreword

I recently had the opportunity to spend four days on retreat with Jason Gant, several of our youth ministry staff, and a group of our senior high youth. I enjoyed observing firsthand the principles Jason articulates in this book.

Jason and the youth ministry staff at The Church of the Resurrection are a remarkable and gifted team who bring together years of ministry experience. They are joined by tremendous volunteers who serve faithfully and sacrificially not only to reach out to nonreligious and nominally religious teens but also to the many youth who have grown up in our church who are well along in their faith journey in order to help them become deeply committed Christians.

This ministry guide captures many of the key insights and "best practices" of Jason and his team. I only wish when I was serving my first church as a part-time youth director that I had had this guide!

If you find this guide helpful you would also enjoy attending, and bringing your volunteers, to The Church of the Resurrection's annual Leadership Institute. The institute includes an entire section of workshops for youth ministries. For more information visit the church's website at www.cor.org.

* * * *

At The Church of the Resurrection, we live daily with the goal to help people become deeply committed Christians. More than nominally religious. More than the Sunday pew holder. More than the spectator. We know these same people become more by doing more. We begin with the knowledge that people want the church to be theirs. They want to know God has a place for them. With that in mind, we recognized from the very start that specialized ministries utilizing the skills and talents of laypeople are fundamental to church life.

A church on the move will have specialized ministries capitalizing on the skills and talents of laypeople. They are your keys to succeed.

In developing these guides, we listened to the requests of smaller churches for practical resources to enlist laypeople for this purpose. These economical guides, written by proven leaders at our church, will serve as essential resources for innovative, creative, and, more than likely, nontraditional church workers who have little or no budget to work with. With these guides in hand, your laypeople will be ready to plunge into the work with excitement and courage instead of tentatively approaching it on tiptoe.

At the core of these guides is the belief that anything is possible. It's a challenge, but it's a truth. God can and does use us all—with that conviction we bring hope to the world.

—Adam Hamilton
Senior Pastor
The Church of the Resurrection
Leawood, Kansas

Let's Take a Trip

Think journey—new experiences, new sights, and new friends. Also think detours, interruptions, constant surprise—and now you're talking a youth ministry journey!

Youth ministry is a rip-roaring, staying-up-all-night, smelly-van, tear-filled-prayer, belly-laugh, caring-heart, listening-ear, goofy-song-motion, deep-question, strong-hug, water-balloon, late-night-worship, pie-in-the-face, exhausting, and exciting movement of the holiness of God through the heart, head, and hands of teenagers and the adults who love them! Amen!

The journey of youth ministry is about discovery in all its different forms. You may be an end-in-mind, plan-it-well, accomplish-a-goal type of ministry leader, but you will learn discovery often comes after the mishaps—even disasters— that can and do happen.

Listen to Paul: "Friends, don't get me wrong: By no means do I count myself an expert in all of this, but I've got my eye on the goal, where God is beckoning us onward—to Jesus. I'm off and running and I'm not turning back" (Phil 3:12-14 [The Message]). Hearing these words through the journey context helps us to understand the moment and the movement of God's spirit in ministry. It's giving the okay to veer away from the plan sometimes . . . to be able to think on your feet so that every seeming disadvantage can be looked to as advantage.

With this guide—or think of it as a road map or GPS, if you will—we will look at some tools and strategies of how to do youth ministry if you never have—and some new ideas if you have. And, we will journey together seeking the holiness of Jesus through teens who are looking to you as their servant leader.

CHAPTER ONE

Where Are We Going?
How Should We Pack?

Where are we headed, what is our goal, and what do we need to take? As reflected in Philippians 3:14: "I've got my eye on the goal, where God is beckoning us onward—to Jesus" (The Message).

At The United Methodist Church of the Resurrection, we understand our faith life to be a journey of Knowing, Loving, and Serving God. It's worth repeating: our mission is to build a Christian community where nonreligious and nominally religious people are becoming deeply committed Christians.

This translates directly into the youth ministry and is embraced by staff, lay leaders, and students as our clear purpose ordained by God. We build all of our preparation and planning around this purpose. The following visual is one I like to use as a teaching tool and template for every program or activity we may do.

Journey Model

We clarify whether our event, program, or activity is a head, heart, or hand focus. Some are more than one. By doing this, we continually evaluate how well we are doing at focusing youth toward Christ as the center of life, then moving Christ back out into the teenager's daily life and the world. We look at the balance of the three-parts (knowing, loving, and serving) to know where we need to improve, change, or grow.

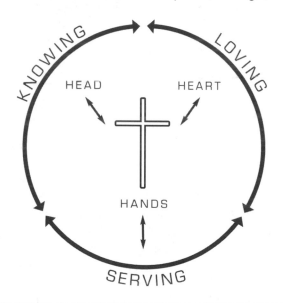

Preparation and Planning for the Trip

Think of **preparation** as the time and energy turned toward God in prayer, listening for the will of God through the Holy Spirit. **Planning** is the equipping needed to change the lives of the next generation.

- Preparation is critical—without it you can become lost.
- Planning takes time and focus.

It is important to note here that planning does not place the Holy Spirit inside of an agenda, but rather frees us to be able to respond in the moment as the Spirit leads.

Preparation: key to beginning the *Retreat* journey

As modeled by Jesus in the wilderness when he faced his own temptations, preparation gave him the strength he needed. You will remember in Luke 4 where Jesus repudiated the devil three times, each time reciting scriptural truths he had learned by heart as a young boy. This passage is so important for those of us who have the privilege to share Jesus Christ with young people. We want to treat this honor with great care and preparation, spending time in prayer and fasting, asking for guidance from the Holy Spirit, and always approaching ministry with young people through humility and authenticity.

Students need preparation modeled. This is where their walk with God and openness to the transforming love of Christ begins; it begins with you, as their servant leader, modeling a life of holiness and humbleness.

Being the first generation to have instant access to the world's information through the Internet, teenagers at this point in time have been exposed to more possible "truths" than ever before. The effect of this seems to be an earnest spiritual seeking, a more honest openness of themselves and who they perceive themselves to be. Connect to any social networking site (MySpace, Facebook) and you will experience it.

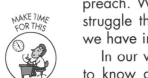
MAKE TIME FOR THIS

As their leaders, we need to practice what we preach. We need to share honestly the areas we struggle through and the moments of celebration we have in our lives.

In our weekly staff team meetings we take time to know and be known, to study, to fellowship, and to pray in preparation to serve God each week. Every Thursday we have a worship service for our entire church staff. Each spring and fall our youth staff members go on retreat together. We do plenty of dreaming, brainstorming, and planning, but we begin with preparation through the Holy Spirit—spending time together fasting, praising God in worship, taking prayer walks, reading from scripture, reciting creeds, and honest sharing of our lives with one another. This is the foundation of the retreat, and this is true across our church-wide staff. Recently on a senior staff retreat we fasted specifically to open ourselves to God's vision and call on our church for the coming year.

Where to begin? Take time and focus

If you're just beginning youth ministry—or reenvisioning—begin by asking for help. Turn to God in prayer and then to your church to include servant leaders. Investing in the lives of key adults and youth to further build kingdom community is what developing servant leaders is all about. This planning is not a place to take shortcuts.

▷ 1. **Meet with your senior pastor** to clearly understand what his or her hopes are for the youth ministry of the church. Know and understand your church's mission and vision. You must begin with this, otherwise the youth ministry can begin to move outside the church's vision unintentionally. Once you have a clear understanding of your church's mission, it's time to gather a team. In the initial vision meetings with parents and youths, you may want to include the senior pastor and/or a supervising leader whom you report to.

▷ 2. **Begin to identify parents, students, and families** to draw into the vision of the youth ministry. Personally invite their involvement. Gather this group together, begin with prayer and listening, and move toward dreaming, dreaming of God's vision through the voices and hopes of those gathered. In these meetings strive to generate excitement of what could be. This is the time for strong lay leadership to emerge. Be careful here—the tendency may be to focus on the past, pointing out critical changes that need to be made. This is important to draw out; however, you will need to determine the health of the conversation. A good rule of thumb is to gauge the negative versus positive comments made. If it turns toward the negative, you have the task of refocusing them again toward the future. Never allow the group meetings to turn toward bashing what has been or bashing the previous leader—fight this with hope, enthusiasm, and encouragement. Remind them that it will be in future meetings where the critical details will be brought out.

An agenda and timeline might be:

Bi-weekly or monthly vision meetings over the first three months with the following questions as a guide:

- Where do we believe God wants this ministry to go?
- What do we believe God hopes and dreams for each student over the course of their involvement in the youth ministry?
- What are some of the principles of faith life we want each student to know and understand through this youth ministry?
- How do we believe God hopes to impact the families and homes of each student involved?
- How do we believe God hopes to impact the community beyond the walls of this church?
- What are ways we can create an environment where each student feels the love of God and has the opportunity to respond to that love?

▷ 3. **Begin to move** from visioning into strategic planning. This is where the "rubber meets the road on your journey," where you're looking with a critical eye at your present programs, gatherings, and curriculum. As you move into this phase with your team, be sure of each member's commitment to accomplishing the vision and seeing through the changes that may be needed with your present model or program. This is a good time for one-on-one meetings with each member of your team to be sure of commitment. I also suggest doing some "benchmarking" of other youth ministries that are 10 to 50 percent larger than your ministry; however, never blindly adopt another ministry's strategy or model. Look closely and glean strategies that your team believes would connect to the growth of your ministry in your particular setting.

An agenda and timeline might be:

Bi-weekly or monthly gatherings over the next three to six months with the following agenda as a guide. Evaluation of each program, gathering, or curriculum up against the church's mission and vision.

- Does this line up with where we are going in our mission and vision?
- Will this particular program, gathering, or curriculum help us accomplish our vision?
- What changes need to be made to our present programs, gatherings, or curricula to line up with where we are going in our mission and vision?
- What programs, gatherings, or curricula need to be stopped or phased out in our effort to line up with our mission and vision?
- What programs, gatherings, or curricula need to added or developed to move us toward the mission and vision?

- Which programs or gatherings are designed for discipleship growth? Which are designed for evangelism?
- Are there programs or gatherings right now dependent upon one person? Why? How can you shift these programs to be shared and owned throughout the ministry leadership?

▷ 4. **Develop** a resource list of what is needed to change or develop the programs and/or curricula. Changes in youth ministry can be very difficult, but when there is a team of invested lay leadership, no one is alone in making the changes. If you are heading the program, bring senior leadership into a clear understanding of the plan. It may involve budget changes, staff changes, and certainly volunteer recruitment and equipping. You may begin to feel some roadblocks as things are changing. Some senior leadership, families, and students who have not been a part of the visioning gatherings might express a bit of confusion. A communication plan is critical at this stage. Enthusiastic, clear words and language will need to be developed and brought out into your community through letters, e-mails, web, blogs, and so on. Begin to speak and teach into some of the new changes or developments throughout parent gatherings, student gatherings, and even the church as a whole. Hold Q & A sessions. Remember, it is better to have people over-informed than under-informed. Strong lay leadership should be emerging—these leaders should be present to answer and share their excitement about God's movement in the ministry!

All of this may feel like an overwhelming task, but remember that even through this process families and young people will be growing in their leadership, investment, and commitment to God. Don't look for excuses. If you're a leader in a small church where you feel all alone, then begin smaller. Gather a team of two to three, shorten the timeline, and address the most critical changes or developments first.

Ongoing programs and gatherings may seem to conflict with new plans. It's usually not possible to stop all programs and gatherings as the youth ministry regroups. If that's the case, lengthen the timeline and make the adjustments you need for your plan. God often works well outside our structured agenda. Remember to allow for the Holy Spirit's nudging.

CHAPTER TWO

Who's Coming Along?

Of course, you're hoping to bring in a good number of youth, and they bring a lot of "stuff" both physically and metaphorically speaking. But, seats for the journey also need to be reserved for a few VIPs—professional staff, volunteers, and young people as leaders. Maybe the ideal situation is that in which the church is large enough to have a youth ministry staff. And maybe not.

Every church, regardless of size, has people who care about youth. I want to dispel the myth that youth workers need to be young and hip. I agree that being younger will give someone an advantage in relating to teenage culture; however, to relate the message of Jesus to young people has nothing to do with age. It has to do with passion. Finding and empowering those with this passion is critical for every church. Your church may not be able to pay a salary for youth ministry staff, but remember that's not the only way to go. It's the passion in people working with youth that really counts!

Professional Staff

In the John Ellas book *Clear Choices for Churches*, a book researching specific trends among both growing and declining churches, Ellas says that churches showing healthy growth had a staff-to-laity ratio of one full-time staff person to every 125 to150 active participants in the church. Specifically to ministry with young people, my suggestion would be a ratio of one full-time youth staff person to every 75 to100 active participants in the youth ministry. One youth worker can effectively know about 50 students and their families' names, while knowing on a more spiritually intimate level around 18 to 20 or so students and their families.

Hiring the right staff, with the right gifting, into the right roles is critical to moving forward in mission and vision. Take the time needed to find the right people. Begin by gathering a team of lay leadership to help the interviewing process. Remember that in ministry, you are not just hiring a position, you are recruiting an example leader. This is true even in "behind-the-scenes" or "administrative" roles. Each member of your team will and should be building leadership teams of adult and student volunteers. They will have the greatest opportunity for mentoring others in your particular church.

At Resurrection, we require each staff member to sign a covenant that holds staff accountable to growth in personal holiness and professional proficiency. All team members have regular check-in meetings with their supervisor and annual evaluations, including a "360 review." This is when each staff member submits names of staff and laypersons to fill out an evaluation of him or her, which is returned to the supervisor. The comments both positive and those suggesting growth areas are then shared with the staff member in the annual evaluation, holding confidential which material was submitted by which person. This encourages continued communication and collaboration across ministry areas of the church and across staff to layperson lines.

I would also suggest annual continuing education opportunities for staff members including conferences, forums, and academic development in youth ministry. This helps broaden a worker's understanding of ministry to young people. Some I would suggest:

- Perkins School of Youth Ministry (at Southern Methodist University)
- National Youth Worker's Convention (Youth Specialties)
- National Youth Ministry Conference (Group Publishing and Doug Fields's Simply Youth Ministry)
- Purpose-Driven Youth Ministry (Saddleback Church in Lake Forest, Calif.)
- Willow Creek Youth Ministry Conference (Willow Creek Community Church, outside Chicago, Ill.)

And, don't discount the growth opportunities in your own communities through secular seminars, workshops, and conferences. I have been to many one- and two-day seminars in the areas of project management, coaching, building a winning team, and dynamic communication that have given me great skill growth.

Adult Volunteers

Would most people step into a volunteer role if they were only asked and given clear instruction? Yes. It seems so easy, yet we might not ask. Here are three possible reasons that as youth ministry leaders we might not ask:

> 1. **Asking for help** says we can't do it. Especially if you're on staff you might be hesitant to call on other adults because you feel "this is my job."

At my first church I had a weekly gathering of forty youth. I did it all: I planned the meal, I led the group games, I led the teaching time, and I led the worship time. I was **Awesome!** Nobody did it better than I did, and the adult volunteers thought I was *super minister*. So much so that they didn't even need to be there. So they stopped showing up. After a few short weeks I had grown the gathering from forty youth and five leaders to twenty-five youth and me! Finally I recognized that I had not shared ownership in the ministry. I had shaped the ministry around me as an individual. It was not centered on Christ. I had proved I could do it, but in the process, I proved to the adults they couldn't—or didn't need to. What a mistake! I shifted gears and developed a team of leaders, both youth and adults, who shared ownership and responsibility in the weekly gathering.

▷ 2. **Asking for help** reeks of desperation, not inspiration. Are you familiar with the following tactics of volunteer recruitment?

- *"We just need warm bodies NOW, or else we will have to cancel . . ."*
- *"If you don't sign up, these kids will be running crazy all over the church."*
- *"If I have to do it, you should have to do it too."*

Who would say yes to any of these? I wouldn't—would you? We need to cast the vision, paint a picture, and empower volunteers not only to serve but also to be a part of something larger than themselves! So, you might say to potential volunteers . . .

- *"Come and be a part of a movement of Christ. I am asking an hour a week from you to help change the world for Jesus—and free pizza to boot!"*
- *"There are young people who are yearning for adults to care for them, to admit to them they don't have it all figured out, but seek to be better believers each day."*
- *"I am not looking for experts! Jesus chose normal people, just like you and me, to carry the hope of the world to the next generation."*
- *"You have gifts, experience, and wisdom these young people need to hear. Will you share one or two weekends a year to help shape their character into that of God's?"*

▷ 3. **Not being prepared** to tell volunteers what we want them to do. Every volunteer role should have a detailed description of what is expected. (See Dan Entwistle's *Recruiting Volunteers*, Nashville: Abingdon Press, 2007). At Church of the Resurrection, we develop our descriptions and update them regularly. We give a folder including a welcome letter, application, and descriptions of each of the servant leader roles. We also share what the volunteer should expect from the youth minister (leader, pastor, or whatever the title). Here are a couple of simple examples of ways this can be defined:

Example No. 1

Once-a-month meal provider is expected to:
- Provide a meal for X number of students to be served at X time

- Collect receipts for X supplies to be turned in (in smaller budgets, you may set the expectation they are to cover costs themselves)
- Stay for program and clean up after

Once-a-month meal provider can expect from the leader:

- A phone call or e-mail reminder one week ahead of time
- A menu of meal options to choose from
- Costs covered (in smaller budgets, you may set the expectation that they are to cover costs themselves)
- Provide two to four student leaders to help with preparation

Example No. 2

Weekly small group leader is expected to:

- Make a commitment of X amount of time (end dates of service, or seasonal breaks, are critical to helping a volunteer say yes)
- Meet with the youth leader fifteen minutes before small group each week to pray for the students and their leading
- Follow provided curriculum (I like to give a "menu" that the leader can choose from and even have the members of the group choose. Sometimes this can be a valuable publicity tool.) For example:

  New small group starting: "Girls of Grace," just for girls discovering why boys are like they are and developing the relationship God wants for you.

  New small group starting: "The Men's Room," talking about guy stuff with guys who have been through it.

- Attend training sessions provided X times each quarter

The weekly small group leader can e
leader:

- Weekly meeting to support,
  communicate any joys and conce
- Curriculum provided ahead of time
- Help with promotion and publicity
  (One of the events we do at Churc
  Resurrection is what we call "Next Step
  Fairs." We set up tables or stations. Young
  ple are encouraged to visit three or four stati
  that look interesting to explore what their ne
  step might be.)
- Sharing of all guidelines, procedures, and bound-
  aries on relational connection with youth

Don't forget the power of inspiration

The more you treat volunteering as an "anointed by
God servant ministry" versus a "warm body filling a
space," the more you will see volunteers become excited
and enthusiastic about serving in ministry. A regular gathering of your leaders encourages great team building, fellowship, and accountability. Inviting them into sharing the
vision, equipping them with the skills needed, and giving
encouragement are the keys to long-term volunteer commitment. And lay leadership is vitally important to the
church of today.

Inviting them into sharing the vision

I often say to the youth ministry team that we should be
always working ourselves out of a job. I get puzzled looks,
mainly from new team members. What does this
mean? All too often we fall into the same line of
thought as the church member who says, "Isn't that
what we pay the youth leader for?"

is charged with leading,
g—Servant Leadership.
the twelve disciples to
it alone and it is not
to be: "The gifts God
les, some prophets,
chers, to equip the
ig up the body of
...ie faith and of the
maturity, to the measure of
ɪ_ph. 4:11-13).

...ie in youth ministry, realize that each of us
...rent gifts: hone in on yours and bring alongside servant leaders who have the gifts that you don't. This can be difficult for some of us who are afraid to admit when we are not gifted in a certain area. Do not see your weaknesses as a personal flaw, but important self-recognition (and reminder to be who you are—remember authenticity is key) as a servant leader.

Equipping them with the skills needed

Everyone wants to know how to do it better. Providing regular training for servant leaders (aka volunteers) is key to their success. Connect with your local nonprofit agencies and school systems. People are much more apt to commit to serving when you can show them a calendar of upcoming training options so they can grow in the skills and confidence they need to serve. You might be surprised how many different training opportunities for those working with adolescents are already out there. Most school systems offer different skill-gaining seminars for local teachers like crisis counseling and building self-esteem. Check out whether church workers could attend.

Set up regular training opportunities inside your own church on subjects such as these:

- A walk-through of polices and procedures: discipline, caregiving, and so forth
- How to lead a small group
- How to share your faith
- Spiritual gifts assessment
- Utilizing prayer in ministry
- Becoming an authentic servant leader (being yourself)

Check with other ministry areas and your pastor about leading some of these trainings. There are great pieces of curriculum available through youth ministry resources such as:

cokesbury.com

youthspecialties.com

simplyyouthministry.com

churchvolunteercentral.com

youthministry.com

Giving encouragement

Encouraging servant leaders must be the youth minister's (whatever the title!) number one job. If youth ministers want to reach more than a small group of youth, they will need to raise up leaders and encourage them to come alongside as fellow youth ministers. This picture of "coming alongside" is very important. Helping them to see themselves in partnership with you in ministry is empowering.

Take volunteers out for coffee or for lunch or go to their home. Know what it is that makes them tick, find out ways in which you can support their servant leadership. Praise them publicly. Hold an appreciation event with wacky awards unique to the youth ministry culture. Have the youth present thank these VIPs for their leadership.

We use nametags and adult leader T-shirts through all of our programs and activities, mainly for safety and security purposes. But it's also a way of bonding. Volunteer leaders should never forget how important they are in the building up of God's kingdom!

Student Leaders

In Mike Ratliff's book *Sacred Bridges: Making Lasting Connections between Older Youth and the Church* (Abingdon Press, 2002) he says this: "Leadership is a sacred bridge, a way of connecting youth even more deeply into faith." This should be our goal in developing the next generation's leaders for Christ. "World changers" I like to call them. I love that term because it reminds us to get beyond the walls of the church. We are called to "go into all the world." Let's be sure to do our best at preparing young people for what they will face as they "go into all the world." They are facing it now. Most young people have had dozens of interactions beyond their own personal community, culture, and country through Internet networking. What I mean is, let's don't teach a Christianity that is always fluffy and happy. Today's generation can't be fooled; they are savvy to the world's ills and to the need for self-sacrifice to bring about change. Let's be sure and bring them the truth in love.

We need to be clear about the truth that Jesus offers us, even though it is sometimes tough to digest. Begin by challenging your students into servant leadership. Challenge them to get involved, dare them to make a difference. Challenge each teenager to live a life that is different from that of much of the world's—to live a life following the greatest radical to have ever existed: Jesus Christ!

Ways to involve students in ministry leadership

I meet weekly with a worship design team. It's made up of students and adults involved in any one of the weekly gatherings. The team is announced regularly as "open," meaning anyone, including students and adult volunteers participating in weekly gatherings, can come. I also specifically seek out students from different schools, cliques, grade-levels, and ethnicities. I want to have students in the meeting who are lifelong believers and students who aren't. We develop the themes for the teaching messages and think creatively about skits, the media to develop, interactive prayer experiences, and other ways to engage students into specific topical teachings coming up.

▷ **Suggestions** to involve students in ministry leadership.

- Offer student surveys of what topics or studies to cover.
- Have a suggestion box available for students to place anonymous input—not high-tech, but it works.
- Hold quarterly or monthly "vision gatherings" where students come, are guided through prayer, listen, and then share God's vision for the ministry through interactive brainstorming. (Do this with adult and student leaders together.)
- Plan annual leadership retreats where you personally invite students you have a feeling should be in leadership. (However, I usually feel this about every single student I encounter.)
- Have students give ideas of what teams may need to be formed to accomplish ministry. (Guidance may be needed here, but be sure they feel they have ownership of the ideas.)
- Seek out structured ways teenagers can serve alongside adult leaders inside of children's ministries, ushering, greeting, or on church leadership committees. (You may think about pairing students up for committees since they might feel more confidence in sharing their ideas.)

Develop a "leadership" or what I like to call a "vision" team of students and adults who regularly meet with the youth minister serving as a kind of board visioning forth the future of God's will for the ministry. The four-step leadership process:

1. I do it, they watch.
2. I do it, they do it.
3. I watch, they do it.
4. They do it.

I use this principle through every program, activity, ministry team, and so on. That's from designing a worship experience to developing a retreat, planning a mission, or giving care to a student. I have found through experience teenagers will respond if you simply set the example. Many times they exceed the expectation we set through our own example. This is the ultimate goal in student leadership development.

Which teenager seems to be "leader likely?"

Think of the apostle Peter as Jesus shaped him in great and humble ways. I have found this is the case whenever I spot "Peters" in the group. I try to learn about them, taking them out for a soda, playing a game of basketball, and most importantly visiting their home to connect with their whole family. Special time is needed when a "Peter" is spotted, but the rewards of ministry impact can be exponential.

As an example, I would like you to read about "Jeremy." Jeremy was incredibly sarcastic, and the other students ate it up. I knew I needed to connect with him: he had the power and the pulse of the group and could choose to use it for evil or for the good of God's kingdom. The choice was not only his, but mine as well.

I called Jeremy's family, asked if I could come by and meet them and find ways in which I could serve their family as their new youth minister. I then asked Jeremy if he'd like to play some pool sometime after school. There was a pizza parlor with a pool table right across the street from the church. (A budget line item to pay for these "one-on-one" times with students is a good way to go. Buying them a soft drink or ice cream goes a long way in building trust.) I asked him to be on my leadership team. His response was rather vague and sketchy—"Why would you want me to do that?"—so I shared with him how I felt his opinion was important and that he would have an opportunity to shape the ministry. He said that was cool.

Jeremy eventually became a model student leader in his school, leading "See you at the pole" prayer each year, heading up the praise band, serving the homeless meals every week, and recruiting many other students to come alongside him. This didn't happen just through prayer and the power of the Spirit, although they played the biggest role. It was also because I acted upon it.

We have two choices when we have students like Jeremy. We can either be threatened by them or be reminded these are the people who influence others. I like to think we want to influence the influencers. Get behind these particular personalities and you may have the awesome opportunity of guiding another Peter!

CHAPTER THREE

Toothbrushes and Other Essentials

You've got to bring along some necessities. A toothbrush. Shampoo. Comb or brush. On the youth ministry journey, there are the same kinds of practicalities. You've got to have volunteer commitments, programs for safety and security, and ways to deal with frustrations—and there will probably be many of those. Here are some ideas that you may find helpful.

Covenant Commitment

I suggest having each volunteer, whether they are committing to one time a year, one hour a month, or leading a weekly group, sign a covenant commitment, and do so after prayer together for the task and willingness to serve. (At Resurrection we have a volunteer covenant that is used by all ministries. This creates consistency of message and unity of servant leadership. You can find this on page 36 of Dan Entwistle's *Recruiting Volunteers* Ministry Guide [Nashville: Abingdon Press, 2007]).

Environment, Safety, and Security

When inviting youth into a gathering, it is critical that the environment be a safe place for them to ask questions, seek care, and feel accepted. The adults interacting with the youth must be background screened and properly cleared for inter-action. This is critical, especially when welcoming youth who are vulnerable because of struggles with self-esteem, depression, or unique family dynamics. We as youth leaders should always place this as the highest priority! There are many different programs and subscriptions you can connect with to do background checks. At Resurrection we have a safety and security team that guides decisions in these matters. I might suggest using one of the following providers:

- Group Publishing offers churchvolunteercentral.com, which is a membership subscription providing many resources for youth ministry, including background checks.
- Protectmyministry.com is another great resource subscription for background checks.

POTENTIAL PITFALL

We absolutely hold the line here. If an adult who wishes to serve refuses to give consent to a background check, we do not allow him or her to serve with children, students, or disabled adults. Also, the senior pastor must be supportive of this policy—this cannot be just a youth minister's duty to enforce. This should be a number one concern in your church and your church's youth ministry.

What do we do if a parent or an adult wants to "check out" the program? We encourage it. Each adult must sign in and out and wear a bright-colored visitor tag on their tour by one of the adult volunteers. This is a great time to recruit more volunteer leaders; however, remember that they haven't been cleared to serve yet.

Relational ministry to students

Relational ministry should be your greatest focus in developing ministry to students; however, it can be mishandled or mistreated. It can sometimes be misinterpreted as believing friendship is key—I would argue that mentorship is key. As adults, we are in the power role when it comes to connecting to teenagers. We must treat this with the utmost care and caution, never allowing our own need for esteem building, love, and attention to take over the careful boundaries we should set in a relationship with young people. Remember that a relationship between an adult and a youth doesn't begin in equal roles in the first place.

Here is a chart to help gauge healthy, Christ-centered relationships with youth. This is, in a nutshell, a good map to follow when working with youth. Be healthy with God first, so that you will be healthy with teens second.

HEALTHY RELATIONAL MINISTRY	UNHEALTHY RELATIONAL MINISTRY
BE A MENTOR	BE A PEER OR FRIEND
LISTEN	TALK ABOVE THE ISSUE
BE AUTHENTIC	HAVE ALL THE ANSWERS—BE A KNOW-IT-ALL
SET HEALTHY BOUNDARIES	YOUR BAGGAGE BECOMES THE CENTER
BE CHRIST-CENTERED	BE "ME" CENTERED
MEET IN PUBLIC PLACES	CREATE SUSPICION BY MEETING IN PRIVATE
ENCOURAGE COMMUNICATION WITH PARENTS	BECOME THEIR SURROGATE PARENT
GENUINELY CARE ABOUT THEM	USE THEIR VULNERABILITY TO FILL A VOID IN YOUR LIFE
SEND CARDS, TEXTS OF PRAYERFUL SUPPORT	COMMUNICATE WITH THEM LIKE A CONFIDANTE
GIVE THEM SPACE	DEMAND THEIR TIME
POINT THEM TOWARD CHRIST	BECOME THEIR "SAVIOR"—EXPRESSED AS: *IF I DON'T SAVE THEM, WHO WILL?*

At one church I served, one adult volunteer connected especially well with the students. However over time, I noticed she was becoming more like a teenager rather than an adult mentoring teenagers. I learned she even encouraged teenage girls to sneak out of their home late at night to meet with her. When I heard of this, I confronted her directly about the rumors. Her response was that the teenage girls needed someone to talk to. Granted, this was a true statement, but there is a more appropriate path to handling that. It was clear that she had crossed over the line of mentor into friend, thinking she and the teenage girls could connect as peers, fulfilling a void in her own life, and then inadvertently or even somewhat intentionally coming between the girls and their parents. She was asked to step out of a volunteer leader role. While a tough situation, something like this needs to be dealt with swiftly and always with the support of the senior pastor and/or other important senior leadership.

Frustrations

In your overnight bag on this journey, you're going to find plenty of frustration as a youth worker. You may not pack it—but it will accompany you all the same.

I can remember being frustrated at what I was unable to accomplish in the life of a young person and venting to the senior pastor. "Why wouldn't God allow me to change this teenager's choices?" That's when the pastor replied, "Jason, your name may have five letters in it, but it doesn't spell

Jesus." What a prophetic response to young people not responding to my agenda. I needed a reminder that it is not my job to be their social worker, their counselor, or their surrogate parent. It is my job to "bring them into the presence of Jesus Christ" as Mike Yaconelli, author and co-founder of Youth Specialties, once told me.

This is the difference between youth ministry leaders and other professionals working with young people. Never forget this or allow your own personal agenda or emotional response to interfere with bringing a young person's life into the presence of Jesus!

Sense of Humor

Don't have a "sense of humor"? Get one. A good laugh at yourself will bring balance to your day and humility to your heart. I can think of countless moments when things didn't go the way I had hoped: a team building game that failed at building team, a lesson I spent hours preparing that completely missed the mark, snapping at a student out of frustration, or a slip of words inside a teaching message. At the end of the day, embrace laughter and humor as a gift from above!

Let the Journey Begin

This is where it gets exciting! You are on the road; the journey has begun. What will you do? Where will you stop? What activities will you engage in? How will you balance the whole experience?

It's important to never undersell the church's purposes because of your own misunderstanding of them. Be sure and meet regularly with the youth ministry team to share in big picture decision-making and ownership. Do remember that no matter the size of your church, you should always have a team with you—that must remain a priority.

Will You Create Programs with an In-reach Focus or an Out-reach Focus?

Who are we trying to reach? That may seem to have an obvious answer: any young person between the grade-levels of X and X. But you have to ask yourself, your church, and your team this question of will you have programs focusing on in-reach or out-reach.

This can create enormous tension among the church leadership and the parents. Create a program or gathering focused on drawing the "not yet Christian" and it may be seen as shallow. You may get more youth to come, but where will they gain an understanding of what it means to be a disciple of Jesus Christ? Create a program or gathering focused on biblical study alone and you may not reach the number of youth you are expected to.

My answer would be that you should create both—with a stronger emphasis on outreach and evangelism. This balance can be very difficult to achieve. So, how does the church—and the youth ministry team in particular—achieve balance? Be prepared to keep an eye on the road signs—slow down for curves, yield when necessary, watch for potholes!

Here are two stories from my own experience where I failed at creating that balance. So, two examples—one leaning too far to outreach, one with the focus too inward.

Story # 1: Gatherings that are too shallow never go deep.

When I came to serve at one church as the director of High School Ministries, the church had gone over six months without a high school director and only one gathering was still alive for high school students in the church. There was a small committed group of parents who were holding together the weekly gathering of high school youth, which had fewer than twenty kids. This was a very large church, with over three thousand members, and only twenty kids a week? However, another program, a monthly event designed to reach marginalized high school kids drew over three hundred. This program was absolutely owned by a group of high school leadership youth. They planned it and ran it. They were amazing in their efforts! They were reaching many "on the fringe" kids in the area. Some youth were even heard on their phone, saying

"Mom, I'm at a church . . . I'm not lying!" However, this program was not without problems.

There were mornings after the event when empty beer bottles and cigarette butts were found on church property. This did not fare well, especially since the event was on the Saturday evening before Sunday morning worship services. A clash of cultures you might say. It was also pretty obvious that the church was not having success at bridging these kids into the weekly youth group gathering, which had become a more "exclusive" church-kid kind of thing.

In retrospect, I realize a major problem was that what was being built were two separate youth ministries with two separate constituencies, and with two separate missions. This is an unhealthy, disjointed way of doing ministry. If there is no unified, purpose-filled mission, then a ministry will fail.

What was needed was a bridge to move students not only into the life of the church but also into the life of discipleship. The monthly event had become completely secular, which is not all bad—after all that's who we were trying to reach—but somehow it became "uncool" to move in any element of spiritual formation.

Eventually circumstances allowed for both to be re-visioned and re-birthed by a group of youth with a unified mission and vision. The youth ministry leaders helped in communicating a message to the church about reaching marginalized youth and building the bridge for these teenagers into the larger life of the youth ministry and the church.

Story # 2: Gatherings that seem exclusive are exclusive.

Picture kids really *into* a Bible study: lengthy sessions, theological debate, and a dedicated group. At this church, I saw youth making great strides toward spiritual formation.

Then it came crashing down. Through the *"youth vine,"* I heard that this study was seen as exclusive. The impression out there was that I had personally invited the youth who were a part of it, and it was closed to anyone else. This was, of course, not the case, but because I failed to regularly communicate the vision of this gathering, people drew their own conclusions. The lesson to be learned is to make sure the church as a whole—including information going outside—knows this is a gathering for ALL youth.

A few ideas on how to send information out to make sure everyone finds out about the gatherings: weekly e-mails, mailers, Facebook messages, personal invitations, mass texting, and incorporation of events and programs into your teaching regularly—a kind of "preaching the announcements."

Creating an environment for outreach:

▷ **With dedicated space,** be sure the area where you plan to focus on the teaching, worship, and prayer is free of territorial furniture. (Couches, bean bags, and even pillows—"hang-out" type furniture—can be used as long as the gathering space is separate from it.)

▷ **Recruit and enthusiastically support** youth to serve as greeters with the challenge of seeking out new people to welcome them in (not pointing them out, but instead walking them around under the radar, kind of like recruiting for college athletics—make them feel as if they are the missing player for your team).

▷ **Don't point new people out individually** in front of the whole group; instead take time to have a one-on-one moment, and remember the youth's name—write it down if you have to. (The next week, with a greeting by name from you and other leaders, he or she will no longer feel like an outsider.)

▷ **Introduce yourself** each time you begin to speak to a group or gathering. (Do this even if you know every youth there. It will become normal and expected; then when there are new youth, they don't feel like they are the only one in the room who doesn't know the adult speaking.)

▷ **Leaders wear nametags.** This gives the youth confidence in knowing your name, and who in the room is designated as a leader. In smaller groups don't have student leaders wear tags since they could be seen as exclusive.

▷ **Create programs** that are fun, interactive, and challenging. (If you are meeting in a church, youth will expect talk of faith and religion, so don't water down the message. The next generation is seeking spiritual truth so be authentic!)

▷ **Collect their information** for future communication. (An example might be: "Fill out this info card and get a free soft drink.")

Now that you have created a "not yet Christian" friendly environment, how do you bring them along in the journey toward discipleship? This can be accomplished through authenticity (heart), creative-experiential teaching (head), and a challenge to take the next step to serve (hands).

The journey toward discipleship

Give youth both large and small group settings for faith exploration, worship, scripture study, missions, and fellowship. Returning to the head, heart, hands template on page 12 will help visualization.

Offering both large and small group gatherings is very important. Young people respond to different learning settings and styles—don't get caught in the "one size fits all" mentality.

Often as leaders, we will shape a program or event into what reflects our particular learning style. Limiting your programs or events to one type means you will only reach one type of young person.

It is better to develop a broad menu to reach students where they are in their faith life than it is to force them into a particular idea of where we think they are. Allowing them to choose to grow or take the "next step" is an important way to teach any disciple that faith growth is in a great part their own responsibility.

By focusing on heart, head, and hands, those involved in youth ministry can help youth to know that discipleship isn't about just one area. A full Christian walk will have components of spirituality, scripture, and mission.

The heart

Care for students is the pulse of any youth ministry. Caring adults—volunteers, staff, pastors, parents—who set boundaries with love, encourage students in their faith walk, and point them toward the heart of Christ are essential. It can't be just the youth pastor, or the youth ministry staff, or a couple of volunteers and parents—it has to be full support. Youth ministry, therefore, can't operate in a vacuum.

> ▷ **Have weekly sign-ups** where students can meet one-on-one with a leader. At one church I served we called this "Juice with Jason." There was an "Extreme Juice" store in a strip mall teenagers frequented. I set up 45-minute intervals to meet, listen, and pray. Since it was in a high traffic teen area, it was noticeable and safe. The kids talked with me about school life, home life, joys and struggles. Some came with theological questions and social concerns. Many just wanted someone to listen and pray with them.

> ▷ **Try activity cards.** Hyde Park United Methodist Church in Tampa, Florida, has a great way of

reaching into students' lives. Youth can fill out "come and see me" cards at the info table (these are cards they can fill out with info on their upcoming game, recital, birthday party, or public event so that leaders can show up for support and encouragement). We started doing this and have seen great response from the young people. The table with the cards is intentionally placed at the front of the room to the side so when announcements are made, we can refer to the table. Alongside the "come and see me" cards are sign-ups to meet with a "Rezlife" minister, a weekly take-home devotional, or a pocket New Testament. At the end of the gathering, leaders stand by the table, which the students must walk by to exit, and it creates a great connection point. The cards are then organized and given to the appropriate minister and the event is added to their calendar. We then go and interact with the students, their family, and friends at these events. If we know of a particular relationship with an adult volunteer and student, we will pass on this info to the adult leader so that they may also go.

▷ **Work with your pastoral leadership** to set up support small groups focusing on teen issues such as divorce, loss, esteem, adoption, and so on.

The head

Help the stories of the Bible and the teachings of Jesus come alive. If you aren't passionately seeking God's truth in the Bible, young people won't either. Get creative in the telling of these stories, share historical contexts of Jesus' day, and challenge the youth to apply them to their daily life. Encourage each youth to ask the hard questions. Don't ever be afraid to say "I don't know." Be sure to follow with "I will find out," or even better, "Let's seek this out together." You are not alone in this task of sharing the stories of the Bible and the teachings of Jesus. The resources are at hand: pastoral guidance, sound biblical study tools, and the uncanny power of the Holy Spirit.

By the time many young people have arrived at the youth ministry doorstep, they have come through various stages of Sunday school, Vacation Bible School, and so forth. At this point, they may seem pretty uninterested in the scriptures. So your dilemma is how to spark the interest of the young people and help the scriptures come alive for them. Before doing anything else, begin with prayer. I regularly teach at our large gatherings of youth, but even if I am meeting with a small group, or one-on-one at a coffee shop, I pray this very simple prayer: "God, please let these words be your words and not mine. Keep me here on my knees before you humble and willing to serve. May your spirit of truth speak."

Then I "B.R.I.N.G. I.T."—a formula to create teaching lessons, worship experiences, and small group discussions.

Biblical
Relevant
Interactive
Nominally religious are challenged
Growth
I Pray
Take It Away

It all must begin with a **biblical** base. The next generation wants to hear and understand God's truth, to see the teachings of Jesus expressed and made applicable to their life.

As an example, I taught a series entitled "Being Chosen," drawing out the biblical truth that we are chosen by God.

Even in our sinfulness God wants to use our gifts in unique ways to build God's kingdom. I wanted to bring this concept to life for them, so I used four biblical characters: Moses, David, Mary the mother of Jesus, and Paul. My hope was that each youth hearing these stories would relate to biblical truth in their own experience.

An important point here is that I did not come up with or choose this series alone. I began with prayer and then offered the idea to the worship team, a team of students I meet with weekly to help guide the topics for the teaching lessons. (See pages 28-29.) These youth then helped in choosing the four characters.

The next step is to look at the teaching as being **relevant**. How will this new knowledge impact each student right now? What are ways this teaching can become a part of each youth's story? How is it applicable to each youth's daily life?

I focused on Moses' fear of wholeheartedly following God's call on his life and the ways in which he responds to God with excuses and worry. There are three main reasons we shirk a call from God: 1. We don't think God is speaking to us, 2. We don't believe we are worthy or knowledgeable enough, 3. We refuse to believe a holy God would choose us—an unholy person.

These concepts can relate to all people, especially youth who are struggling with hearing God, their sense of self-esteem and worth, and their recognition of their own sin.

I seek ways through my own story to share the relevance of these truths today. For instance, is God speaking to me? Then I might share a story from my own life experience. Am I worthy enough? Moses himself was a murderer, escaping the wrath of the Egyptian King. God called me by name, knew each hair on my head since the womb (Psalm 139), and sent his son to die for me (John 3:16) so that I would know just how worthy I am to God.

The next piece is where the most creative touches come in, making it **interactive.** This is where we need ways for each learning style to connect with the teaching. I am very visual, so thinking this way is very natural for me. However, I also need to think about the auditory, and the hands-on style of learning. What are ways they can see the concept? Ways they can hear it? Ways in which they can touch it?

If you are in a small group setting, I might suggest acting out some of the scriptural stories through drama, creating a commercial, or a "true Hollywood story" about the character. Develop your own prop box full of funny dress-up clothes, wigs, and items youth can use to express themselves and the truths shown in these stories. Use the medium of paint to express the emotions the characters may have been feeling. This particular lesson is great to build around discovering spiritual gifts. Have the students take a gifting survey or evangelism style assessment. See *Serving from the Heart for You: Find Your Gifts and Talents for Service* (Abingdon Press and Church of the Resurrection, 2007). This has some good assessments you can use and leader and participant guides. Two others are *Becoming a Contagious Christian* (Willow Creek Community Church, Zondervan, 1996 and on) and *Discover Your Spiritual Gift* by C. Peter Wagner (Regal, 2005). Discuss what gifts or style Moses, David, Mary, or Paul may have had.

In a larger setting, develop a drama team that acts out the story as a part of the teaching, or re-create a scene relevant to their context, such as a basketball court where kids are choosing their players, reenacting the feelings of being the last one chosen, or the scene from Matthew 4 where Jesus calls the fishermen. Have students create artwork to display visually the point of the story. Use a responsive liturgy or active prayer about being chosen.

The next two steps are sometimes the most difficult. I want the teaching to speak into the life of **nonreligious or nominally religious** young people and challenge them to **growth.**

This is where the teaching must have an impact! If we are just painting a picture of what was and not bringing truths of how this can change us today, we are just storytelling, and not teaching.

Once I have walked through these steps, I very simply **pray** they will **take it away.** I am cautious never to think it is my creativity or power that teaches these lessons, but the power of the Holy Spirit, always tying in whatever topic or lesson is presented into the life, death, and resurrection of Jesus Christ!

The hands

Evidence of poverty, illness, and despair in our local communities, around America, and all over the world inundate young people. Many seek tangible ways for believers in Jesus to respond, to make a difference in the lives of people and their communities—to serve as the hands and feet of Christ. It is our responsibility to encourage servant leadership, both inside and outside the walls of the church. This begins with personal example. We encourage our students to be in missions, so are we? We encourage our students to be passionate about issues important to Jesus, so are we?

⬭ **Begin** with challenging all adults involved in youth ministry to be serving in some capacity outside the walls of the church. Whether that is volunteering as a tutor through a local school, serving with Habitat for Humanity, or going on an international mission experience, we must be using our hands in missions, if we are going to challenge young people to do so alongside us.

⬭ **Teach** on social justice issues. In Jesus' teachings, he called us to issues of the poor, the widowed, the marginalized. We need to include these teachings in our foundational discipleship development with young people.

49

▷ **Gather** youth together on a team to pray and discern what God's call is on them as the church. Which issue or concern is God calling them to respond to? Maybe the AIDS epidemic, or children in poverty, modern-day slavery, the homeless, or the elderly.

▷ **Encourage** family service days. At Resurrection we participate in what is called "Faith Works," a monthly service day to serve the Kansas City area. Families are invited to come that Saturday morning and join teams to go out and serve in the community. This is a great first step of service.

▷ **Align** mission experiences with the church mission connections. Often times we sign up to do missions with the company that sends us the flashiest brochure or gives us the best price. Don't get me wrong, these are certainly great missions, but the power that takes place when the young people of your church are engaged in the same partnerships as adult missions is amazing. One benefit is a shared experience between a teenager and his/her parents—the fact that they are sharing an issue of response is very compelling to families.

▷ **Share** missional stories inside weekly gatherings. Mission moments bring about the importance of missions inside the culture of your group. Have students give team reports within the youth ministry and all ministries of the church. Different groups of the church need to hear what the youth are engaged in—this preaches and teaches to the congregation as a whole.

CHAPTER FIVE

Unexpected Detours

The bump in the road is where we need to be open to change, course correction, even re-mapping. You know the saying, the "best laid plans." We need to be open to the movement of the Holy Spirit—possibly even more when dealing with young people.

There are common challenges . . .

Challenges in Common:

At one time or another, the dedicated full-time youth worker or the dedicated servant leader will probably encounter some of the following or something like them. You may have to correct your course.

You have irate parents confronting you about advice given to their teenager.

First of all, be sure you are giving good advice. I make it clear that I am not a counselor—I am a listener. I might make suggestions, but I am careful never to overstep my bounds as a youth minister. If this complaint is unfounded or simply a difference of opinion, be sure to involve your senior leadership in the situation. Remember to be humble, listen, and state clearly your hope and direction to the parent. It goes without saying, always pray before going into any discussion with a student, parent, or family.

The volunteer leaders don't show up.

Keeping your volunteer leaders engaged is key to any program. First, never start any new program or gathering where it is dependent upon your attendance. When others share the ownership, they will invest and prioritize their time accordingly. Communicate regularly with all leaders, never assuming they will be there. Know it for sure. Have them share in the leadership: run a game, serve a meal, lead a prayer, give the talk, lead a team-building exercise, and so forth.

Your family tells you they feel they are running second to the ministry.

Talk about a situation that will make your head hurt and your stomach churn! Your desire is to say something like, "I am serving God here, what do you want me to do?" However, don't give in to the inclination to use God to justify an action that may be about your own ego or need to feel needed. The order of our life should be:

God
Family
Ministry
Everything else

Often we mix ministry with God. This may be the most valuable advice I can give you: SAY NO. You are not Jesus, remember? If you are not in a healthy situation with your family, it will be very difficult, if not impossible, to be effective in ministry to a community!

You think you're not cool enough to be with teenagers.

I subscribe to the concept that beginning a life with Jesus starts the moment you decide to make him the Lord of your life. It is in that moment that eternity begins, not at the end of the 70+years. I now walk with Jesus' power and grace, both equally among my life and my impact on the building up the kingdom of God. With this in mind, servant leaders in ministry should recognize that each day, each moment, can become a movement by God. For whatever reason you find yourself in ministry with teenagers, whether you feel called to it or you are exploring a call to it, whether you are a parent or concerned adult who desires to be there for young people, whether you chose this or were nominated by the pastor, whether this is your career or a short-term part-time thing, whether you are paid by worldly means or volunteer in response to God's love for you, know this: youth need caring, loving, guiding servant leaders who will show them God's love in real life—people who will be present, living honestly about their struggles and joys. People who are always seeking to connect their story to God's story.

You think you're too awesome for youth ministry.

See above.

CHAPTER SIX

Are We There Yet?

W hat a question. It can feel like we spend our whole life wondering if we've made it. Have we finished the job? Have we completed the task? Is the journey over? The question may have to do with whether our youth ministry is successful. Do we have good programs? Good numbers? Are we doing things the way they should be done? You can answer yes to all of these but still need to keep in mind an important concept for young people. This concept comes from a good friend of mine in ministry who recently shared his mother's wisdom with me that is far beyond any formula, strategy, or program any of us could ever hope to develop on how to minister to teenagers. I suggest reading the next five words slowly and twice over.

"Be Present . . . Just Be Present"

When we think back on our formative years, I would imagine each of us could point to one or two individuals who were pivotal in our spiritual development. It may have been your parent, a relative, an athletic coach, dance instructor, guidance counselor, teacher, or family friend. For me it was a pastor. I am sure to this day he doesn't even realize the impact he had on me. But he showed what being present—really present—was to me. When he arrived new to our church, I was forced by my parents to accompany them to welcome him to town. I did everything I could to remain in the driveway shooting basketball. However, he came out and played with me. He met me where I was, truly caring about me and wanting to get to know me. My parents never really even noticed while they were meeting his family in turn, but you can be sure they saw my approach to church changed for the better.

Never Underestimate the Power of Being Present

Mike Yaconelli (see page 37) also told me, "The interruptions are the ministry." I will never forget it. And it should rock all of us spiritually and consciously as we take stock in our ministries. How often we do not recognize the needed interruption or are too busy, scheduled, or task-minded to see the opportunity for ministry standing right in front of us.

If you've been in youth ministry a while you may remember a similar experience to the following examples—or to a missed opportunity. If you're just getting involved in youth ministry, keep these in mind.

For a group

- The Thursday night following 9/11 my church at the time held a prayer service. The sanctuary was packed, candles were lit, and a community of believers came together in a time of fear and uncertainty. It was a moving worship experience. I had to leave the service a little early to go to another building when I received a call on my cell phone. It was one of our church leaders telling me that a group of young people had stayed after the service and were looking for someone to answer their questions. The leader then told me, with some trepidation in his voice, "Jason, some of them have pink hair." As I arrived in the sanctuary, the group of young people was sitting patiently as the ushers were cleaning up through the pews. I welcomed them and stated my name and what I do at the church. One girl responded, "We know who you are." I asked how they knew me. I started listing every program or church ministry we had for youth. Worship? Youth group? Sunday school? Small groups? Ministry teams? They replied no to each one. They came each month to our nontraditional outreach that showcased local bands. When I asked them what brought them here this night, they responded, "This is our church." I can remember the feeling of the Holy Spirit working through that moment. They came seeking answers to questions we all had after that tragic event. Where was God? Why did this happen? I can remember feeling so honored to be the voice of grace on behalf of Jesus Christ to these young people. We cried together, prayed together, and developed an unexpected relationship that carried on well past that particular night.

For one

• "Karen" was thirteen years old when her parents went through a difficult divorce. I connected with Karen many times throughout her teenage years in a mentoring, spiritual support role. There were times she was full of doubt about God. I would be available to listen, to pray with her, and to continually encourage her to lean on Jesus in tough times. Karen became a leader in the church, helping to start home cell groups, run worship and behind the scenes tech ministries, and she even preached on Youth Sunday. She told how the church had been her rock through her parents' divorce, a place of refuge through a difficult time of her life. She was honest about her struggles and obstacles, but through it all learned that God loves her.

- I received a call from my senior pastor that "Jim's" dad had committed suicide. We went to Jim's home to be there when his mother told him. As we gathered together in the living room and the news was shared, I recognized my presence was what I could offer Jim. I wanted him to know I was there for him—that God was there for him. When I asked him if he would like to take a drive to get out of the house, he responded, "I need to run, will you run with me?" It was about eight at night and we started jogging. Not a word was said, just two guys running side by side. When we stopped, not a word was said for what must have been an hour. I can remember going over that night, struggling with what I should have said. It was weeks later when Jim said to me, "I am really glad you were there that night at my house. You were really there for me." It wasn't at all about any theological perspective I could have shared, or what words I could have used to comfort him. It was very simply my presence, my being there through a terrible tragic night of Jim's young life.

The need for young people to have present, caring adults in their lives is there whether you are a church of 100, of 1,000 or of 10,000. It's all about the "one" in this moment. I believe that God has called individuals with specific passions and gifts to be present in their lives in every congregation. It is our job to seek them out and offer them ways to be present in young people's lives.

Making Room for More

I know your ministry will be blessed if you are earnestly seeking God with all of your life. God may even bless it if you're not. Somehow God always seems to take our shortcomings and bring them forward into God's will!

Adding People

When your church's youth ministry grows toward adding staff, start researching staff structure of churches at the next ministry level. What works well? What doesn't? What can you glean from their structure that will work in your particular context? What gifts do you have? What are the other gifts you need on your team?

▷ **Strongly consider** college-age internships. This is a great way to bring new energy into your team.

▷ **Structure** by giftedness versus grade level in the beginning. This creates a larger team concept across the ministry.

▷ **Consider:** Administrative support positions will never seem as important as relational positions; but these positions help lay foundations of communications and procedures critical to a ministry's success.

> ⇨ **Know:** The key in staffing expansion are these: strong music, media development, and leadership.

Evangelism Tactics

Creating a culture of evangelism is critical to growth both spiritually and numerically. (Don't be afraid to count, keep records, and evaluate them. Somebody counted at Pentecost!)

> ⇨ **Lead** by example. When is the last time you invited someone to church? Spent time sharing your testimony? Offered a listening ear in the name of Jesus?
>
> ⇨ **Create** events that are nonthreatening at places where teens are comfortable (movies, bowling lanes, basketball courts, and so forth).

Discipleship Tactics

> ⇨ **Develop** an overarching curriculum of what you hope students have learned in the six to seven years in youth ministry. There are great curriculum resources out there offering just that.
>
> ⇨ **Remember** disciples are not made by trendy ideas, programs, system models, or fancy media. Disciples are made by other disciples. Begin by being present and teach others to be present!

Utilizing Technology in Youth Ministry

Technology is the means to connecting with the next generation. Music, media, and the Internet should be inside your message, lesson, and events. Remember when Jesus went to the fishermen, he connected and talked about fishing. When he went to the farming community, he connected and taught

through illustrations relevant to farmers. Reaching teenagers means connecting and talking through the things that are relational to and relevant in their life!

Technology has brought a new shape to how I do ministry. It may look a little mind-boggling if you're not part of the electronic generation. My best advice? Get the kids involved and you will have excellent tutors.

• I used to send e-mails. Now I have set up groups through networking sites like Facebook to reach kids instantly with information (e-mail to this generation is like "snail mail" is to mine).

• I used to say *call me*. Now I say leave a post or message on my Facebook and I am instantly sent the message on my mobile phone via the web text feature.

• I used to post responses to questions during a teaching session by a previously made PowerPoint® slide. Now I use a free resource like wiffiti.com to have kids text during the message their response and it automatically posts on screen (it even has a rating system, so nothing vulgar gets through).

• I used to print out pictures of our activities and post them on bulletin boards (I still do, even though it's so "low tech"). Now I developed a free flickr.com account and shared the upload password. Students upload dozens of pictures from their summer camp or retreat experience to share with our community.

• I used to ask kids to create a skit, and still do. Now I more often will ask them to develop a video to share on a subject or event coming up.

• I used to send out newsletters. Now I do a weekly parent e-mail and a daily blog using a free resource like blogspot.com and even video log (I

make short videos up to around two minutes from the camera I carry in my pocket) certain announcements and events I want shared with the community.

CLOSER LOOK

- I used to pass out index cards for surveys. Now I post polls online and get a much better response.
- I used to collect payments and forms (some you still have to) for retreats and camps by hand. Now I use a resource like poweredbyyou.com (there is a cost associated here) to do all electronic registrations and payments for retreats, camps, confirmation, small groups, and events.

One thing I used to do—and still do—is send handwritten notes and postcards. So, don't get so caught up in technology that you forget to be personal in your interaction. With that said, it is important that each of us research what is new to reach and teach students in their world. If you feel really lost here, then put a team of students together and brainstorm ways they think the ministry can use technology.

Networking

Getting connected to the larger youth worker picture in your community will not only help you with ideas, but keep you sane. Consider local youth workers and youth ministry agencies—connecting about issues, concerns, and questions is great!

Pray

Pray each day that your will doesn't move in front of God's will. This will be my prayer for each of you. I hope you will return the same prayer for me. So let's get going with the hope and prayer that we have to make room for more. After all, life here is just the beginning of the real journey.